Music That Teaches English!

Original Songs
Games
Creative Activities
by
Patti Lozano

with Audio-Cassette

For Beginning
English students at
all grades levels

Dolo Publications, Inc.
Language through Music

Copyright ©Patti Lozano 1999
All Rights Reserved
First Printing 1999
Second Printing 2003
Printed in the United States of America

ISBN 0-9650980-6-0

This publication is protected by Copyright and permission should be obtained from the publisher prior to any prohibited reproduction, storage in a retrieval system, or transmission in any form or by any means, electronic, mechanical, photocopying, recording or otherwise. Permission for duplication, however, is granted to the individual teacher for any portions of the book that will benefit the student in his/her classroom.

Dolo Publications, Inc.
18315 Spruce Creek Drive
Houston, Texas 77084
Toll free: 1-800-830-1460
fax: (281)679-9092 or (281)463-4808
Email: orders@dololanguages.com or plozano@sbcglobal.net
www.dololanguages.com

Acknowledgements...

Heartfelt thanks go to...

my husband Alberto for listening to and evaluating each word, line and verse of these songs many times and for withstanding my outspoken suffering in good humor, (to say nothing of fixing my computer on a regular basis!)

to my three sons, Ari, Johnny and Jesse, for their interest and support, and for singing these songs around the house of their own volition... thanks also to my sons for performing on the audio cassette; Ari, age 13, played the drums, Jesse, age 7, and Johnny, age 11, sang solos.

to my mother for her constant support, endless enthusiasm and editing endeavors!

to my friend, Jan Caviel, for her considerate musical talents on the keyboard, and to her son, Alex, for his solo... thanks also to Ruben Perez and Sara Blummer for their solos.

to all the ESL and bilingual teachers who requested this book and have given me suggestions and ideas as to what they need for their students.

Other works by Patti Lozano
(Published by Dolo Publications, Inc.)

Music that teaches Spanish!
More music that teaches Spanish!
Music that teaches French!
Music that teaches German!
Leyendas con canciones
Mighty Mini-Plays for the Spanish Classroom
Mighty Mini-Plays for the French Classroom
Mighty Mini-Plays for the German Classroom
Mighty Mini-Plays for the ESL Classroom
Get Them Talking!
Spanish Grammar Swings!
French Grammar Swings!
Teatro de Cuentos de Hadas
Latin American Legends: on Page, Stage & in Song (Spanish version)
Page, Stage & Song: Latin American Legends(English version)
Skinny Skits

Contents

I.   Introduction .... i – iv

II. Teacher's Guide .... v – viii

III. Songs, Games and Activities, Templates and Flashcards ... 1a – 15d

   1. Hello, Good Morning to All my Friends! *(Greetings)* ... 1a, b, c, d
   2. What is Your Name? *(Introductions)* ... 2a, b, c, d
   3. ABC Like Candy Cane *(Alphabet)* ... 3a, b, c, d, e
   4. The Classroom *(Classroom objects)* ... 4a, b, c, d
   5. Draw a Square *(Common commands in the classroom)* ... 5a, b, c, d
   6. I Have an Itch *(Body parts)* ... 6a, b, c, d
   7. What are You Going to Wear Today? *(Clothing)* ... 7a, b, c, d
   8. I'm a Bird of Many Colors *(Prepositions)* ... 8a, b, c, d
   9. Pass the Salt to Me, Please *(Family members, courtesy, food, table settings)* ... 9a, b, c, d
   10. In Mississippi *(Rooms, furniture, U.S.A. states)* ... 10a, b, c, d, e
   11. Tick Tock *(Daily routine, telling time, verbs)* ... 11a, b, c, d
   12. Orange Juice *(Food and drink, "I like..."/"I don't like....")* ... 12a, b, c, d, e
   13. Two Lazy Elephants *(Leisure activities, question words and phrases)* ... 13a, b, c, d
   14. Oh Irene, Don't Be Mean, Tell Me Please *(Personal hygiene)* ... 14a, b, c, d
   15. I Want to See the World in a Fine Purple Car *(Transportation, adjectives)* ... 15a, b, c, d

IV. Teacher Guide to Activity Guide Templates and Flashcards ... 16 - 18

Introduction

" **Music that teaches English!** " is a comprehensive song and activity book for learners of English as a Second Language, that reinforces basic topics and is guaranteed to create fun for its users. Music enhances language acquisition for both beginning and intermediate students of English as a Second Language. The fifteen songs contain commonly used vocabulary and structures, presented in a motivational format. Teachers will share their students' enthusiasm as they -

...sing original songs
...learn useful vocabulary in entertaining context
...discover meaning through illustrations
...take part in creative activities to reinforce learning
...play games to reinforce retention

Although the text has been directed primarily towards elementary and middle schools, all ESL teachers who want to add a new dimension to their instruction will find it useful. The author has provided an *audio-cassette* and *reproducible pages* to facilitate student learning. To facilitate duplication further, all pages have been printed on one side only. *The audio-cassette may not be reproduced.*

Recent research by educators and scientists, such as Eric Jensen and Howard Gardner, has identified music as one of the less-tapped learner intelligences. When used on a regular basis, along with other effective learning strategies, music helps students increase their capacity for learning and helps them retain whatever they have learned. Music, visual props, rhythms, choreography, games, role playing, improvisation, and open-ended hands-on activities become motivational tools that make learning fun and help students develop vocabulary, grammar, and communicative skills.

The author, who is an accomplished composer and musician, as well as a language teacher, has included a number of these strategies to accompany each of the songs to allow the teacher to integrate music into everyday teaching. The book has been designed to make teaching of songs an enjoyable experience for both teacher and student. Even the students' parents will want to learn the songs.

Kids love to sing! The original tunes and lyrics found in this book will encourage them to want to learn the English language. You will hear tunes reminiscent of the rock'n roll 50's, and the swinging 60's, as well as rhythms and melodies that evoke the music of Mexico and South America.

Why are these songs different?

• each song meets one or more teaching objectives found in most
     beginning and intermediate English textbooks

- the author of the book is the composer and illustrator. She is also an experienced music and language teacher as well as an instructional video personality

- the song arrangements consist of voice, guitar and a variety of musical instruments; all are fun to listen to and sing along

- the vocabulary is simple and fun to learn

- the tunes and lyrics are catchy and repetitive and tend to "grow on you"

- the topics include the alphabet, greetings, the home, the classroom, body parts, telling of time, hygiene, leisure activities, clothing and others.The author also has addressed some topics that require special effort to hold the students' attention, , such as grammatical forms including conjugations, prepositions, and descriptive adjectives, as well as structures

- the Table of Contents includes a brief description of the topic addressed in each song

Book Format

This song and activity book has been designed to be "teacher-friendly." As indicated in the Table of Contents, the book is organized as follows:

I. Introduction -

The why's and how's of the book

II. Teacher's Guide -

Explanation, strategy suggestions and useful activities for incorporating music into the English as a Second Language curriculum.

III. Songs

Each song contains pages that follow an easy-to-use "a,b,c,d" (and occasional "e") format.

A. Page a: The song is transcribed with musical notation and guitar chords: This page will enable teachers who play the piano, guitar or autoharp to accompany their students. Students who play instruments will appreciate a copy of this page. Lyrics to all verses of the song are also included here.

B. Page b: This is an important teacher guide and lesson idea page. It contains three sections.

I. Language objective box: A box encloses both vocabulary and structural objectives. Examples are given and targeted vocabulary is listed.

2. Games and activities: Three to six creative games are designed to extend the vocabulary and structures identified in each song. Games are often related to activity templates and flashcards found on the "d" and "e" pages of that song.

3. Modify the song: This section offers ideas for enhancing and extending the targeted vocabulary and structures by modification of the song. There are suggestions for improvisation, role-play, changing and much more.

C. Page c: This illustrated song page is for the students. All song lyrics are illustrated so that students and teachers can follow the content of the song by recognizing the vocabulary via drawings. The teacher is encouraged to duplicate this page so that all students will have a sheet. If every "c" page in the book is copied, then each student will have a personal illustrated songbook! Teachers may also choose to enlarge this page as a transparency to use as a visual aid.

D. Page d: All activity templates and flashcards are found here: All flashcards or visuals necessary to play the creative, open-ended inter-active games and activities suggested on page b are found here. There are game boards, telephones, "radios," vocabulary cards and much more. The combination of singing and hands-on materials is a team that can't be beat for retention of language vocabulary and concept!

* * * *

This song and activity book has been created by Patti Lozano with love and understanding for young people who are trying to learn a new language. The composer/author has worked with children of varying ages as her models and has sung with them in classrooms, social settings, in large groups, and in small groups. Her background as elementary music teacher and her numerous contacts with elementary and secondary teachers as presenter and master teacher has given her a thorough understanding of what "turns kids on." When she meets a group of students, feet begin to tap, hands begin to clap, bodies sway with the music, and voices ring out. . . and, most important, children learn the music and English.

I hope that this song and activity book will give you, the teachers, as well as your students, as much pleasure as it has given me in creating it.

Patti Lozano

iv

Teacher's Guide

Incorporating music into the curriculum is a joy for both the teacher and the student. Music alone provides a powerful incentive for learning. Coupled with motivational instructional activities, it effortlessly builds vocabulary for communication, locks in retention, and instills a subconscious understanding of language and culture.

On the following pages a number of activities are introduced that have proven successful in classrooms where music has been an integral part of the curriculum. You may already be familiar with a number of these, but hopefully some of these activities will be new to you. We have tried to stay away purposely from pedagogical terminology because the book may be used by laymen as well as experienced English as a Second Language teachers.

A great deal of research has been conducted during the past few years about multiple intelligences inherent in all human beings by such experts in the profession as Howard Gardner, David G. Lazear, and Eric Jensen). Music and rhythm rank high among the seven identified intelligences described below. Our *stick figures* will help you identify these intelligences.

- **Verbal/Linguistic** -
  Relating to words and language, both written and spoken

- **Logical/Mathematical** -
  Dealing with thinking, reasoning, numbers, and recognition of abstract patterns

- **Visual/Spatial** -
  Thinking and visualizing images and pictures

- **Music/Rhythmic** -
  recognizing tonal patterns and environmental sounds; learning through rhyme, rhythm, and beats

- **Body/Kinesthetic** -
  Relating to physical movement; includes the brain's motor cortex which controls bodily motion

v

- **Interpersonal** - Learning through person-to-person, group relationships, and communication

- **Intrapersonal** - Learning through self-reflection and liking to work alone

Where do you fit? Where do your students fit? We have observed students at various grade levels in classrooms and have found that information presented via song is not only enjoyed by all, but information is retained more quickly. The voices, the tapping of the feet, the clapping of hands, role-playing gestures, and the sharing among the students all play an important part in retention.

Try the various activities described in this Teacher's Guide to achieve maximum benefit of the songs in this book. The activities are not listed in order of importance. Any one of them can be selected when needed or when the teacher wants to emphasize certain segments of a song.

Most of the activities achieve the highest degree of success when they are used orally. English as a Second Language teachers know that language is acquired first by listening, then speaking. The reading and writing proficiencies follow. In this text we suggest that the written activities, which follow each song and rhyme, be used for reinforcement only after the song has been learned.

Following are some of the best-recognized and successful activities used in second language classrooms to encourage language learning:

1) **TPR - Total Physical Response** - consists of simple commands given by the teacher and followed by the students. The pattern is as follows: a. The teacher models the command without expecting response from the students; b. the students respond to the command as a group; c. commands are given to individual students by the teacher; and d. students give the commands to each other. This method sets a pattern for the class and is useful for everyone of the songs contained in this volume.

Ex: "Orange Juice" (Song #12) deals with foods. After singing the song and achieving familiarity with the foods described, the teacher points to the food item on a flashcard (Activity Page 12d) and says: "Touch the orange juice!" The students follow the example. They can become more creative as more commands are added, and as more vocabulary is added. Some of the most useful commands are listed here. You can add more as the students progress.

Give me . . .	Ex. Give me the orange juice!
Give him . . .	Ex. Give him the orange juice!.
Touch . . .	Ex. Touch the orange juice!
Look for. . .	Ex. Look for the orange juice!
Put . . .	Ex. Put the orange juice on the table!
Walk!	
Sit down!	
Stand up!	

2) **Acting out** - in skits, pairs, or alone; this may be done in the form of pantomime when students repeat the actions called for in the song Ex. "I'm a Bird of Many Colors" (Song #8) - students point to bird in the direction requested

3) **Pairing** - asking two students to speak to each other Ex."Oh Irene, Don't Be Mean, Tell Me Please!" (Song #14) - students break into pairs and take the parts of Bartholomew and Irene

4) **Adding more verses** - using diverse or extended vocabulary Ex. "I Want to See the World in a Fine Purple Car" (Song #15) - add as many different modes of transportation as students are willing to sing

5) **Flash cards** - Ex. "The Classroom" (Song #4) - use flash cards to identify classroom objects

6) **Poster-size songs** - any song can be enlarged so that students can follows the lyrics more closely. Caution: Use only after song has been learned orally

7) **Change target vocabulary** - to create new meaning Ex. "What is Your Name!" (Song #2) -switch pronouns and names of students, personalizing the song.This is also a great way for students to learn grammar painlessly

8) **Play games** - a favorite is Simon says . All students know that one, regardless of age. It may be used with any of the songs. Relays and cumulative verses are popular also

vii

We are sure, as creative teachers, you can think of many more activities, but these can be used as starters. Check the Teaching Suggestions and Activity Page which follow each song for additional suggestions.

Now . . . you are ready to go. Is your audio-cassette player ready to play? We suggest the following sequence:

* Play the song while your students listen

* Play it again (hold up visuals when available)

* Play the song a third time, asking the students to sing along

* Give the students the illustrated song which you have duplicated for them. They should each have their own copy. With young children, suggest they look at the illustrations to understand meaning. Older students can identify the target vocabulary and try to read the verses

* When the song and vocabulary have been learned, suggest they practice English with games and the illustrated activity page found after each song

Practice makes perfect! When you include a song in each of your lessons, students will love your ESL class! Good luck!

a. Songs with Musical Notation, Guitar Chords and Lyrics

b. Language Objectives, Games and Activities

c. Illustrated Song Lyrics

d. Activity Templates and Flashcards

1. Hello, Good Morning to All My Friends!

Words and music by Patti Lozano

Hello, Good Morning to All my Friends!

Hello! Good morning to all my friends
Hello! Good morning to all my friends
Hello! It's so nice to see you here
Hello! Good morning to all my friends

2. Hello! Good afternoon to all my friends...
3. Hello! Good evening to all my friends...
4. Goodbye! See you later and have a nice day...

1a

1. Hello, Good Morning to All My Friends!

Teaching Suggestions

> **Language Objectives:**
> ☺ Become comfortable singing together
> ☺ Common greeting and farewell expressions

Extension Games or Activities:

A. Show magazine photos that display various daily activities. Students guess which greeting(s) would apply in each situation.

B. Have students mill around the room greeting each other. They greet as many friends as they can in a three minute period, never using the same greeting twice in a row.

C. One student pantomimes activities; the others guess which greeting is appropriate here.

D. Play "Greetings:" Choose a pose to represent each greeting/farewell, (i.e. a shining sun with both hands held high for "good morning," the classic baseball bat swing position for "good afternoon," rubbing sleepy eyes for "good evening" and a wave for "good bye") Students all stand in a circle with one leader in the middle. As the leader points to each child around the circle and says a greeting/farewell, each student assumes the predetermined position. When the leader points to a student and says "So long!" then that student becomes the new leader and the game begins again.

Modify the Song:

A. Use students' names in place of some lyrics.
   Example: *"Hello, Good morning to Raquel and Juan...."*

B. Play "The Radio Game" <u>only</u> when students are quite familiar with all lyrics: when the radio is "on" (see page 1D for radio template), the students sing out loud. When the radio is "off," the students sing only in their heads, always keeping a soft beat with two fingers. When the radio is turned on again, everyone should sing out loud in the <u>same new</u> place in the song.

C. Learn to sing the song in sign language.

D. Brainstorm more greetings and farewells. Use them in place of the original lyrics to create new verses. Some possibilities include: *Hi! What's new? How's it going? How are you? It's really great to see you today! Bye bye! So long!* (Be aware that some little clown in your classroom will suggest "*¡Adiós, amigos!*")

1. Hello, Good Morning to All My Friends!

Hello! Good morning to all my friends
Hello! Good morning to all my friends
Hello! It's so nice to see you here
Hello! Good morning to all my friends

Hello! Good afternoon to all my friends
Hello! Good afternoon to all my friends
Hello! It's so nice to see you here
Hello! Good afternoon to all my friends

Hello! Good evening to all my friends
Hello! Good evening to all my friends
Hello! It's so nice to see you here
Hello! Good evening to all my friends

Goodbye! See you later and have a nice day!
Goodbye! See you later and have a nice day!
Goodbye! It was so nice to see you here
Goodbye! See you later and have a nice day!

1. Hello, Good Morning to All My Friends!

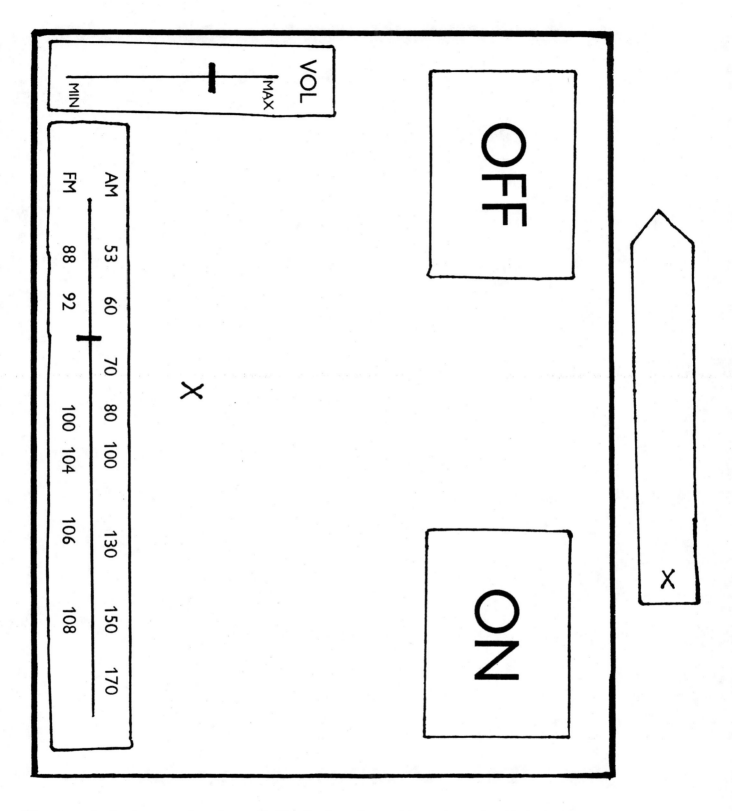

Directions: 1. For best results enlarge this "Radio Game" template and copy it on index stock.
2. Color the "off" rectangle red and the "on" rectange green.
3. Cut out the arrow indicator, color it brown
4. Attach the arrow indicator to the front of the radio by inserting a brad through the "x" at the end of the arrow and through the radio at the "x" mark
5. Color the tuning band if you wish. Your radio is now ready to play any song!

2. What is Your Name?

Words and music by Patti Lozano

What is Your Name?

What is your name? My name is Jesse.
What is your name? My name is Jesse.
What is your name? My name is Jesse.
My name is Jesse and I like it a lot!
His name is Jesse and he likes it a lot!

Is it Jess-a-lini? No, it's not!
Is it Jess-a-rama jama? No, it's not!
Is it Jess-a-chuga wuga? No, it's not!
My name is Jesse and I like it a lot!
His name is Jesse and he likes it a lot!

2a

2. What is Your Name?
Teaching Suggestions

Language Objectives:
- ☺ Learn classmates' names
- ☺ Develop confidence speaking/chanting or singing alone
- ☺ Vocabulary/Structures: *What is your name? My name is_____. His/her name is____. Is it____? Yes, it is. No, it's not.*

Extension Games or Activities:

A. After students are very familiar with the song, allow volunteers to solo on the "My name is Jesse" part. Make a transparency of page 2C and black out Jesse/Sara/Alex so that students can insert their own names.

B. Copy a name card for each child using the template on page 2D. Give the students time to draw their own features in the faces, then bend the cards and set them up..
   1) Ask students at random, *"What is your name? Is it_____?"* and encourage them to answer correctly. Let student volunteers ask the questions.
   2) Brainstorm additional rhyming nonsense syllables to attach to students' names.
   3) Instruct the students to draw cartoons of famous people or comic strip figures on their name cards. Students guess who the drawing is *(i.e. Q: "Is it Spiderman?/ A: No, it's not.")*

C. Play "Blind Handshake:" Invite 5 students to the front of the room. Student A shakes each person's hand as you introduce them and describe their hands as well, *(i.e. Her name is Roberta. She has a small hand. She has long fingernails. She is wearing a ring.")* Then blindfold Student A. As the other four students shake hands again, student A tries to correctly identify the name of each handshaker.

Modify the Song:

A. Chant the song lyrics instead of singing them.

B. Use a repeating rhythmic pattern under the chant or song. The pattern should repeat after 4 beats. Some suggestions:
   1) Pat knees, clap, pat knees, clap
   2) Pat knees, clap, snap, clap
   3) Pat knees, hit right elbow, pat knees, hit left elbow

2. What is Your Name?

What is your name?   My name is Jesse.
What is your name?   My name is Jesse.
What is your name?   My name is Jesse.
My name is Jesse and I like it a lot!
His name is Jesse and he likes it a lot!

Is it Jess-a-lini?   No, it's not!
Is it Jess-a-rama jama?   No, it's not!
Is it Jess-a-chuga wuga?   No, it's not!
My name is Jesse and I like it a lot!
His name is Jesse and he likes it a lot!

2. What is your name?   My name is Sara.
   What is your name?   My name is Sara.
   What is your name?   My name is Sara.
   My name is Sara and I like it a lot!
   Her name is Sara and she likes it a lot!

   Is it Sar-a-lini?   No, it's not!
   Is it Sar-a-rama jama?   No, it's not!
   Is it Sar-a-chuga wuga?   No, it's not!
   My name is Sara and I like it a lot!
   Her name is Sara and she likes it a lot!

3. What is your name?   My name is Alex.
   What is your name?   My name is Alex.
   What is your name?   My name is Alex.
   My name is Alex and I like it a lot!
   His name is Alex and he likes it a lot!

   Is it Alex-a-ini?   No, it's not!
   Is it Alex-a-rama jama?   No, it's not!
   Is it Alex-a-chuga wuga?   No, it's not!
   My name is Alex and I like it a lot!
   His name is Alex and he likes it a lot!

2. What is Your Name?

What is your name?

My name is

_____ .

3. ABC Like Candy Cane

Words and music by Patti Lozano

ABC like Candy Cane

ABC like candy cane
D and E like emu egg
We can sing the alphabet in English, We know how!
F and G like girl and gem
H and I like insect
J and K, L and M, then comes N like number

O and P like pumpkin pie
Q and R like raindrop
We can sing the alphabet in English, We know how!
S and T like tiger tail
U and V like violin
W like windowpane, X Y Z like zebra

3a

3. ABC Like Candy Cane
Teaching Suggestions

Language Objectives:
- ☺ Learn the letters of the alphabet
- ☺ Learn the sounds the letters make

Extension Games or Activities:

A. Pipecleaner games are fun, creative and irresistible. Give each student a new pipecleaner from a multi-colored pack. Try some of these activities:
  1. Say a letter; students bend the pipecleaner to form that letter.
  2. Say a word with a short vowel sound: students form the pipecleaner into the vowel sound they hear.
  3. Say a word: ask students to form either beginning (or ending sound) with their pipecleaner.
  4. Allow students to form the letter of their choice. They must think of a word that begins with that letter. Let them share their letters and words.
  5. Allow students to form the letter of their choice. Graph them according to color and letter name. *(i.e. "How many pink "M"s are there?")*
  6. Place students in groups of 3. Say or show a flash card of a 3-letter word. Groups work together to see who can form the word first.
B. Use the letter templates on pages 3D and E to play various word formation games. Give each child a complete set of letters and instruct them to cut the letters apart.
  1. "Word formation:" The teacher says a word or shows a picture and the students form that word with their letters.
  2. "Bat Sat Cat:" Give the students a word such as *"bat"* and have them see how many rhyming words they can create by changing out the first letter.

Modify the Song:

A. After the students are very familiar with the song, having charted page 3C from a transparency, black out the words the letters make (i.e. *"ABC like XXXXXX"*) and have students brainstorm other words that will fit. Note: the replacement word should have the same number of syllables as the original word in order to fit the best. For example, *"clever cow"* sounds much more pleasant when sung than *"car."*
B. Sing the alphabet with letter sounds instead of letter names. (Sing the short vowel sounds.)

3. ABC Like Candy Cane

A B C like candy cane   D and E like emu egg

We can sing the alphabet in English, We know how!

F and G like girl   and gem   H and I like insect

J and K, L and M, then comes N like number

O and P like pumpkin pie   Q and R like raindrop

We can sing the alphabet in English, We know how!

S and T like tiger tail   U and V like violin

W like windowpane,   X Y Z like zebra

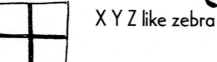

3. ABC Like Candy Cane

f	l	r
e	k	q
d	j	p
c	i	o
b	h	n
a	g	m

3. ABC Like Candy Cane

x	o	t
w	e	s
v	a	r
u		p
t	z	n
s	y	l

4. The Classroom

Words and music by Patti Lozano

4. The Classroom

The classroom, the classroom,
What do you have in the classroom, the classroom,
What do you have in the classroom, the classroom,
What do you have in the classroom?

In the classroom there's a pencil
Every classroom has a pencil   (2X)

2. chalkboard
3. teacher
4. table

4a

4. The Classroom
Teaching Suggestions

Language Objectives:
☺ Vocabulary: classroom objects such as *pencil, chalkboard, teacher, table*
☺ Structures: *"What do you have....?" "There's a ...."*

Extension Games or Activities:

A. Play "Mystery Bag": Hide one or more classroom objects inside a canvas or cloth bag. A student must feel the outside of the bag and guess how many objects are inside and which objects they are. After the guess the student looks inside to see if he is correct. The student then pulls each object out of the bag and shows it to the class while naming it.

B. Play "Pass the Tray": Put many different classroom items on a large tray, (such as a calendar, large and small scissors, 5 different color crayons, a glue stick, a long and short pencil, etc.) Set a timer for 3 – 5 minutes. The students pass the tray around. As each student gets the tray, he must describe one item and take it off the tray, *(i.e. "There is a short, yellow pencil.")* How many items can be described and taken before the timer dings.

C. Make a transparency of page 4D to play "To Say or Not to Say": Point to an item and make a statement. If the statement is correct, the students repeat it. If the statement is incorrect, the students remain silent.

   Example: Teacher: *I write with the scissors.*
   Students: *No response (only giggles)*
   Teacher: *I write with the pencil.*
   Students: *I write with the pencil.*

Modify the Song:

A. Use the same melody with different lyrics, *(i.e. "The desert, the desert.... What do you see in the desert, the desert"....etc... "In the desert there's a cactus....")*

B. Create a cumulative song. With each verse add an additional classroom item. It's more tricky than it sounds, therefore have students stand in front of the class to hold up each item as it is sung.

   Example: Verse 1: *In the classroom there's a clock...*
   Verse 2: *In the classroom there's a clock and a table...*
   Verse 3: *In the classroom there's a clock and a table and a map...*
   Verse 4: *In the classroom there's a clock and a table and a map and a desk...*

4. The Classroom

The classroom, the classroom,
What do you have in the classroom, the classroom,
What do you have in the classroom, the classroom,
What do you have in the classroom?

In the classroom there's a chalkboard
Every classroom has a chalkboard
In the classroom there's a chalkboard
Every classroom has a chalkboard

In the classroom there's a teacher
Every classroom has a teacher
In the classroom there's a teacher
Every classroom has a teacher

In the classroom there's a pencil
Every classroom has a pencil
In the classroom there's a pencil
Every classroom has a pencil

In the classroom there's a table
Every classroom has a table
In the classroom there's a table
Every classroom has a table

4. The Classroom

5. Draw a Square

Words and music by Patti Lozano

5. Draw a Square

Well, I draw a square, then I draw some more
I draw squares in the air and squares on the floor
I draw squares on myself and squares on my friend,
'Til my teacher says, "STOP! This is the end! Yeah, yeah, yeah!
You there – SIT DOWN IN YOUR CHAIR!"

I like my teacher, I really do
And I always try to do what she asks me to do
She says, "Draw a square. It will make me glad."
So I draw a square so she won't be sad.

2. Write your name
3. Clap your hands
4. Color with blue

5. Draw a Square
Teaching Suggestions

Language Objectives:
- ☺ Describing school day activities such as, *"I draw a square, I write my name"* etc.
- ☺ TPR (Total Physical Response) commands

Extension Games or Activities:

A. Play: "The Action Chain Game"; Divide students into teams of 6 - 9 students and have them sit in rows. Each player thinks of a command he will give when it is his turn. It may be a simple command *(i.e. "Jump ten times")* or a complex command involving several steps, *(i.e. "Hop to the window, touch it with your nose and say your name")*. All rows begin at the same time. The first student gives a command to the second student. The second student performs it and then gives a command to the student, and so on. The first row to finish wins.

B. This is a dynamite role playing song. Choose one child as teacher and let everyone else play the carefree role of the "teacher's challenge" student. When the cassette/child teacher says, *"You there – SIT DOWN IN YOUR CHAIR!"* everyone must immediately sit quietly to wait for the next verse to begin.

C. Page 5D is a game board of many daily classroom activities. It may be used in many ways:
1) Make a transparency of it and play "Fly Swatter." Give two students fly swatters and have them stand on each side of the screen. When you name the action, the first student to swat the correct picture wins a point. The first student to receive 5 points (with 5 you can keep the score of each player on your fingers) wins and is ready to accept a challenger.
2) Play "I'm Not Doing It!": Show the transparency, but copy one class set of page 5D cards on index stock as well, enlarging them if you wish. Distribute one card to each student. Have students sit in a circle with their cards plainly visible. Student A announces that he's not doing what's on his card, but (looking at the transparency if necessary,) that he's doing a different activity. Whoever has the activity he names gives Student A his card and the game continues with the new student.
    Example: Rico (who holds the "draw a square" card): I'm not drawing a square. I'm cutting out a star."
    Su Lan (gives Rico the "cut out a star" card): I'm not cutting out a star. I'm I'm reading a book."

Modify the Song:

A. Let the students brainstorm more everyday classroom activities. Make a list of them on the board. Try singing and role playing them. (Some will work better than others.) Take a vote on the favorite new verse.

5. Draw a Square

I like my teacher, I really do
And I always try to do what she asks me to do
She says, "Draw a square. It will make me glad."
So I draw a square so she won't be sad.

Well, I draw a square, then I draw some more
I draw squares in the air and squares on the floor
I draw squares on myself and squares on my friend,
 Til my teacher says, "STOP! This is the end! Yeah, yeah, yeah!
You there – SIT DOWN IN YOUR CHAIR!"

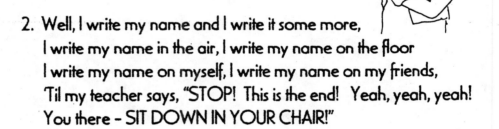

2. Well, I write my name and I write it some more,
 I write my name in the air, I write my name on the floor
 I write my name on myself, I write my name on my friends,
  Til my teacher says, "STOP! This is the end! Yeah, yeah, yeah!
 You there – SIT DOWN IN YOUR CHAIR!"

3. Well, I clap my hands, then I clap them some more,
 I clap my hands in the air, I clap my hands on the floor,
 I clap my hands on myself, I clap my hands on my friend,
  Til my teacher says, "STOP! This is the end! Yeah, yeah, yeah!
 You there – SIT DOWN IN YOUR CHAIR!"

4. Well, I color with blue, then I color some more,
 I color in the air, I color on the floor,
 I color on myself and I color on my friend,
  Til my teacher says, "STOP! This is the end! Yeah, yeah, yeah!
 You there – SIT DOWN IN YOUR CHAIR!"

5. Draw a Square

6. I Have an Itch

Words and music by Patti Lozano

6. I Have an Itch

I have an itch on my face (3X)
And I don't know what to do!
2. Nose
3. Lips
4. Ears
5. Hair
6. Neck
7. Shoulders
8. Arms
9. Hands
10. Fingers

6. I Have an Itch
Teaching Suggestions

Language Objectives:
- ☺ Body part vocabulary: *face, nose, lips, ears, hair, neck, shoulders, arms, hands, fingers.*
- ☺ Structures: *"I have _____." "I don't know what to do!"*

Extension Games or Activities:

A. This cumulative song is an activity in itself! Play the song on the cassette and tell the students they must remember to scratch the designated body part *and* sing the lyrics *at the same time*. At the end of each ever-longer verse there is an eight- beat guitar interlude, during which they may dance in any frenzied manner they wish. At the end of the guitar interlude they must freeze to be ready for the next verse.

B. Draw a "Picasso." Have three 3-ft. pieces of butcher paper hung length-wise along the walls for this activity. Explain a bit about the famous artist Picasso. If possible, show one of the artist's famous abstract paintings. Now blindfold three students, lead each to a "canvas" (butcher paper) and give each a marker. Students will draw according to your directions. You might say,

> *"First draw a lady's oval head. Now draw long hair. Now draw a graceful neck. Give her two small ears with pretty earrings. Now draw her big beautiful eyes. Draw a flower in her hair. Now draw her lovely mouth..."*

When the drawings are complete, artists take off their blindfolds and admire their work as the class titters. Review the body parts on the drawing. .Very entertaining and lots of fun!

C. Make one class set of body part cards from page 6D and distribute one to each student. Play "I See a Horrible Monster!" The teacher says dramatically,

> *"I see a horrible monster - and he has no eyes!!!"*

The student holding the "eyes" vocabulary card stands and says with equal drama:

> *"Yes! I see the monster too. He does have eyes - but he has no _____!"*

The game continues, the tension grows. Give a prize to the most dramatic speaker.

Modify the Song:

Have the students instruct you to draw a human figure on the board. Label and number the body parts in the order the students want to sing them. Now you have a totally new version of the song!

6. I Have an Itch

I have an itch on my face
I have an itch on my face
I have an itch on my face
And I don't know what to do!

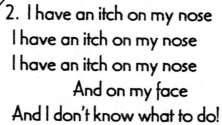

2. I have an itch on my nose
I have an itch on my nose
I have an itch on my nose
    And on my face
And I don't know what to do!

3. I have an itch on my lips
I have an itch on my lips
I have an itch on my lips
    And on my nose
    And on my face
And I don't know what to do!

4. I have an itch on my ears
I have an itch on my ears
I have an itch on my ears
    And on my lips
    And on my nose
    And on my face
And I don't know what to do!

5. Hair   8. Arms

6. Neck   9. Hands

7. Shoulders    10. Fingers

6. I Have an Itch

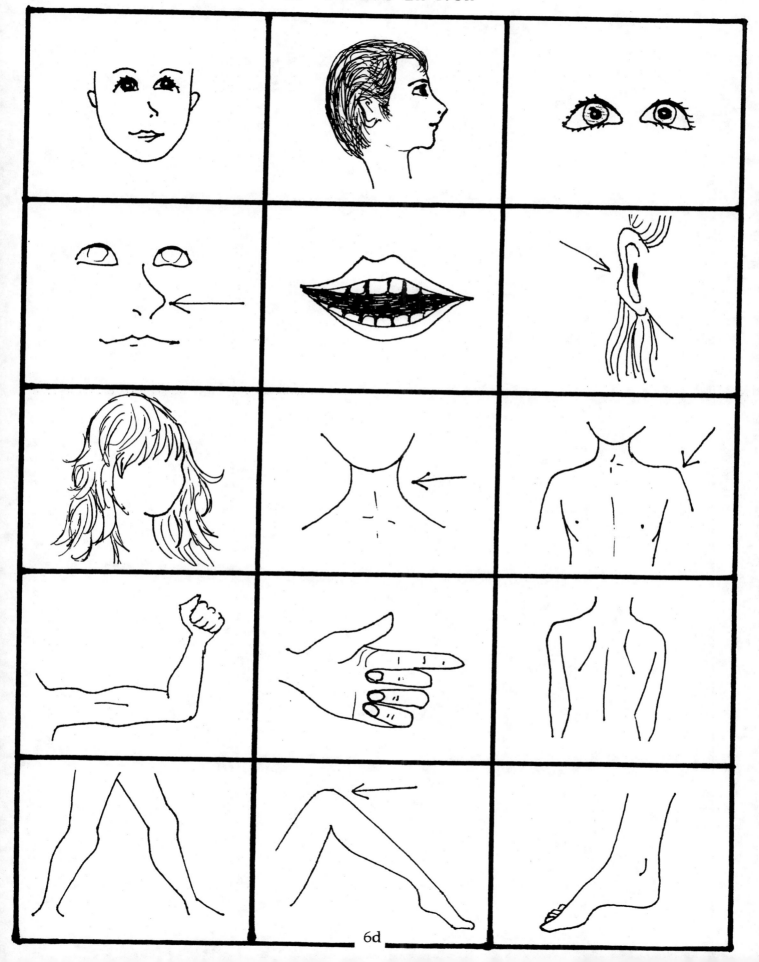

6d

7. What are You Going to Wear Today?

Words and music by Patti Lozano

7. What are you Going to Wear Today?

Rise and shine, the weathers' fine
What are you going to wear today?   (2X)

I am going to wear my shirt   (3X)
But first I'm going to sleep some more.

2. My pants
3. My socks
4. My shoes
5. My jacket

7. What Are You Going to Wear Today?
Teaching Suggestions

Language Objectives:
- ☺ Clothing vocabulary: *shirt, pants, socks, shoes, jacket*
- ☺ Structures: *"What are you going to wear today?"* *"I am going to wear my ___."*

Extension Games or Activities:

A. Play a fast-paced "Clothing Relay:" Divide students into groups of 6 or 7 and have them sit in rows with a laundry basket at the front of each row. Each basket contains similar items of clothing in large adult sizes (i.e. every basket might have a pair of socks, a pair of pants, a shirt, a sweater, a pair of shoes and a skirt.) To begin the game, the first person on each team stands and announces, *"I am going to wear my shirt"* or *"I am putting on my shirt."* As soon as the shirt is on, the student takes it off, saying either *"I am not going to wear this shirt."* or *"I am taking off my shirt."* The first student then hands that item of clothes to the person behind him. That person begins with the shirt while the first student begins with another item of clothing. The first team to complete the putting on/taking off cycle wins.
Important! Teams may use the clothing in their basket in any order. Also, every team member must say the key phrases or the item goes back to the first student!

B. Use the vocabulary cards on page 7D to play "The Lottery." Make a set of cards for each student. Each student chooses his three "lucky" cards and puts the rest away. The teacher chooses three cards as well, and announces the clothing items on the cards to the class. All students who have the same three cards are winners! They jump up and scream, *"I won!"* Be sure to have small prizes on hand. If there are no winners in a round (and there often aren't,) let the same 2-out-of-3 cards win.

C. Play "Police, police!" The whole class stands in a circle. Two students stand In the center playing the roles of the parent and the police officer. The object of the game is for the police officer to "find" the lost child according to a clothing description. The lost child is a classmate who the parent has already silently chosen. The dialogue goes like this:
Parent (wringing hands frantically): *Help! Help! My child is lost!*
Police (with authority): *Calm down, ma'am/sir. What is your child wearing?*
Parent: *My child is wearing blue pants!*
Police: *Is this your child?* (Chooses student from circle)
Parent: *No, my child is wearing blue pants and black shoes.*
The dialogue continues until the police identifies the correct child. The police and parent choose students to take their places and the game continues.

7b

7. What are You Going to Wear Today?

Rise and shine, the weathers' fine
What are you going to wear today?
Rise and shine, the weathers' fine
What are you going to wear today?

1.
I am going to wear my shirt
I am going to wear my shirt
I am going to wear my shirt
But first I'm going to sleep some more.

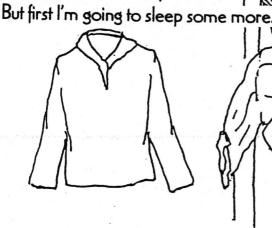

5.
I am going to wear my jacket
I am going to wear my jacket
I am going to wear my jacket
But first I'm going to sleep some more.

2.
I am going to wear my pants
I am going to wear my pants
I am going to wear my pants
But first I'm going to sleep some more.

4.
I am going to wear my shoes
I am going to wear my shoes
I am going to wear my shoes
But first I'm going to sleep some more.

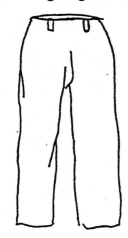

3.
I am going to wear my socks
I am going to wear my socks
I am going to wear my socks
But first I'm going to sleep some more.

7. What are You Going to Wear Today?

8. I'm a Bird of Many Colors

Words and music by Patti Lozano

8. I'm a Bird of Many Colors

I'm a bird of many colors, prettier than the others
Watch me as I fly through the lovely blue sky   (2X)
I'm over it (echo)   I'm under it (echo) 2X
I'm happy when I'm flying but I'm sad when I'm inside (echo) inside (echo)
I'm sad and cold, My cage is old

2. Near/ far   3. Above/below   4. In front of /behind

8a

8. I'm a Bird of Many Colors
Teaching Suggestions

Language Objectives:

☺ Prepositions: *inside/outside, over/under, near/far, above/below, in front of/behind*

Extension Games or Activities:

A. Duplicate the bird template from page 5D on index stock to make a class set and allow students to color them with markers. Mount each bird on a popsicle stick. Several activities may be played with these birds:
> 1) Give TPR commands telling students what to do with the bird.
>> Examples: *"Put the bird on your head. Put the bird under your desk." Put the bird near the window.")*
> 2) Choose four students to come to the front of the room with their birds. Describe the arrangement of birds that you desire using prepositions and colors. Students arrange birds according to teacher's description.
>> Example: *"The bird with the red head is near the bird with the yellow head. The bird with the blue wing is under the bird with the yellow head. The black-tailed bird is far away."*
> 3) Let students, in groups of four, create their own bird arrangements and take turns describing them to the class.

B. Build a Lego structure. Divide students into groups of three. Give each group a baggie of assorted Lego pieces. They work together to build a structure following the teacher's directions.
> *Variation:* Place students in groups of three and give each student a baggie with ten Legos. Each group sits together, back to back so that they can't see each other's Legos. One child calls out commands as he builds a structure. The other students attempt to create the same structure by following the commands. When the structures are completed, the group compares them. They will be similar, but not identical due to differences in Lego shapes and colors.

Modify the Song:

Most popular activity! Choreograph the song with the colored bird templates (page 8D.) Each free-spirited "bird" must choose a partner to be the dreaded cage with curved arms of steel and interlocked fingers! Looks like a bird chorus line!

8b

8. I'm a Bird of Many Colors

I'm a bird of many colors, prettier than the others
Watch me as I fly through the lovely blue sky
I'm a bird of many colors, prettier than the others
Watch me as I fly through the lovely blue sky
1. I'm over (echo)   I'm under (echo)
   I'm happy when I'm flying
   But I'm sad when I'm inside (echo)
   Inside (echo)
   I'm sad and cold, My cage is old

3. Above/below
4. In front of /behind
1. Over/under
2. Near/ far

(I'm sad and cold, My cage is old)

8. I'm a Bird of Many Colors

9. Pass the Salt to Me, Please

Words and music by Patti Lozano

All of my family is in the dining room,
Sitting at the table, they want to eat their food
They open up their napkins and then pick up their spoons
When I say, "Stop! Pass the salt to me, please"

And Mother passes the salt, and father passes the salt,
And Grandma passes the salt
They all have to wait, this is great!
Now my aunt passes the salt and my uncle passes the salt,
My cousin passes the salt, and finally my brother now passes me the salt!

Coda: I'm in my room all alone.

2. Bread
3. Grapes

9a

9. Pass the Salt to Me, Please
Teaching Suggestions

Language Objectives:
- ☺ Family members: *mother, father, grandma, aunt, uncle, cousin, brother*
- ☺ Courtesy expressions: *please, thank you, you're welcome*
- ☺ Structures: *"Pass the ___ to me, please."*
- ☺ Related activity: Setting the table, naming tableware and foods

Extension Games or Activities:

This song tells a story starring the youngest son of the family. Every time the whole family is ready to eat, the mischievous little boy asks for something to be passed down, person by person, from mother to him — at the other end of the table! All following activities deal with this meal.

A. Set the table with a "Table Setting Chain:" The teacher, at one end of the room, has a tablecloth and 8 table settings. At the opposite end of the room is the "dinner table." Six to eight students line up between the teacher and the table. The teacher passes the table cloth to the first student, saying, *"Please put the tablecloth on the table."* Each student passes it to the next with the same command. The last student places it on the table, saying, *"I am putting the tablecloth on the table."* Follow the same procedure for all place settings (or until all students have had turns.)

B. Fun! Fun! Fun! Role play the song/story. Give each family member a prop/disguise to show who they are (perhaps a necklace for mother, a tie for father, a shawl for grandma, a silly hat for uncle, and so on). Play the cassette as students act out the story. IMPORTANT! Students <u>must</u> <u>not</u> pass the food until they hear their character's name! Each character *must* remember to say *please, thank you* and *you're welcome!*
Note: Use a real salt shaker, taped, so the salt won't pour out. Also use real bread and grapes, so that students can actually put some in their plates or bowls.
Note: Video tape the final performances!

C. Don't take off those disguises! Add "grandpa" and "sister" to the table. Set various foods (see page 12D) or plastic foods on the table. Play "Pass the Food Politely:" Mother begins by requesting a family member of her choice to pass a certain food to her *(i.e. "Grandma, pass the potatoes to me, please")*. The passer then becomes the requester and the game continues. Don't forget to say *"Thank you"* and *"You're welcome!"*

9. Pass the Salt to Me, Please

All of my family is in the dining room,
Sitting at the table, they want to eat their food
They open up their napkins and then pick up their spoons
When I say, "Stop! Pass the salt to me, please"

And Mother passes the salt, and father passes the salt,
And Grandma passes the salt
They all have to wait, this is great!
Now my aunt passes the salt and my uncle passes the salt,
My cousin passes the salt, and finally my brother now passes me the salt!

2. Bread
3. Grapes

All of my family is in the dining room,
Sitting at the table, they want to eat their food
They open up their napkins and then pick up their spoons
But I'm in my room all alone.

9. Pass the Salt to Me, Please

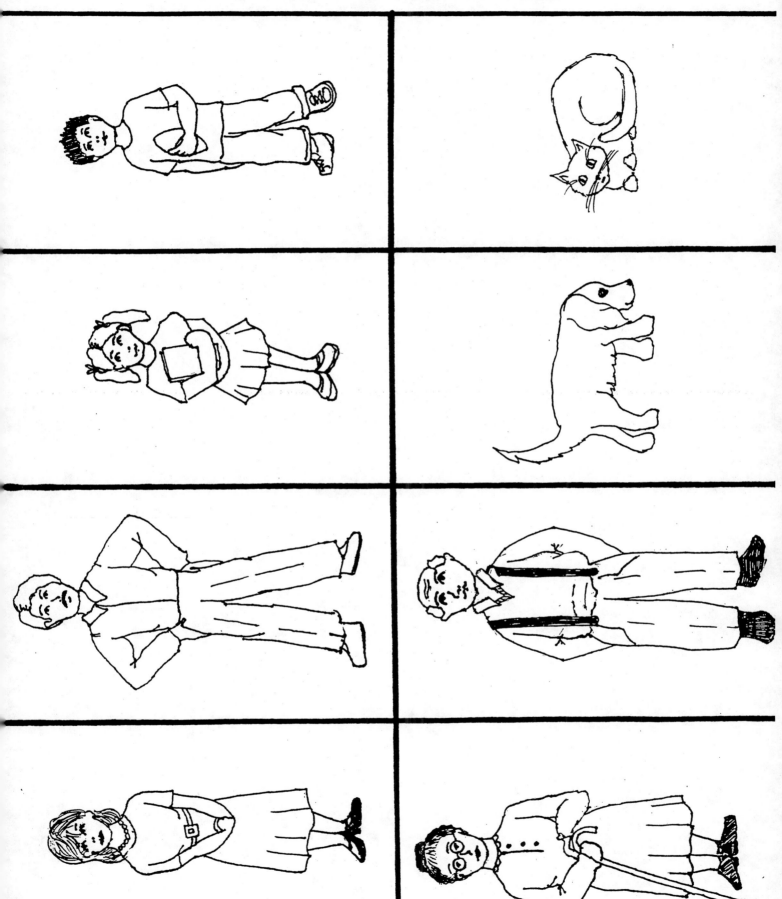

9d

10. In Mississippi

1. In Mississippi Skippy has a kitchen with a stove (3X)
   Well, the house has a kitchen and the kitchen has a stove
   Is the stove in the kitchen?   Yes, it is.
   Is the stove in the bathroom? No, it's not.
   Is the stove in the kitchen?   Yes, it is.
   Yeah, the house has a kitchen and the kitchen has a stove

2. In Arizona Mona has a bathroom with a sink (3X)
   Well, the house has a bathroom and the bathroom has a sink
   Is the sink in the bathroom?   Yes, it is.
   Is the sink in the bedroom?   No, it's not.
   Is the sink in the bathroom?   Yes, it is.
   Yeah, the house has a bathroom and the bathroom has a sink.

3. In Alabama Ana has a bedroom with a bed
   (Is the bed in the den?   No, it's not.)

4. In North Dakota Rhoda has a den with a couch
   (Is the couch in the kitchen?   No, it's not.)

10. In Mississippi
Teaching Suggestions

Language Objectives:
- ☺ Rooms of the house: *kitchen, bathroom, bedroom, den*
- ☺ Furnishings: *stove, sink, bed, couch*
- ☺ States: *Mississippi, Arizona, Alabama, North Dakota*

Extension Games or Activities:

A. Copy the house and furnishings (page 10D) and the family members (page 9D) for each student. Let students "decorate" (color) the house, as well as color and cut out the people. Many house/furniture/family activities can be played with these cut-outs.

1) Instruct students where in their houses to place all family members.

2) Place students in pairs. Student A directs Student B where in the house to place all family members. They may make it serious (*i.e. "Put the lamp in the bedroom"*) or silly (*i.e. "Put the dog on top of the lamp"*).

3) Write a short descriptive paragraph about a family in the house. As students listen, they place figures in the correct places. When the paragraph is completed, have the students retell where everything is. Now say the paragraph again, but change several characters and locations. Students must look at their houses to tell you what is different! (Try creating a mini-mystery story!)

Modify the Song:

A. What a great improvisation song that teaches about the United States and rhyming at the same time! Have students think of new verses using different states' names and girl/boy names that rhyme with them. (Girl/boy names may be quite creative and unique.) Locate all these states on a map. Write the key words of the new verses in the states.

B. Choreograph this song. Any pattern of movements that move with the beat will work. Copy page 10C for everyone and record choreography with stick figures near the lyrics where they occur.

10. In Mississippi

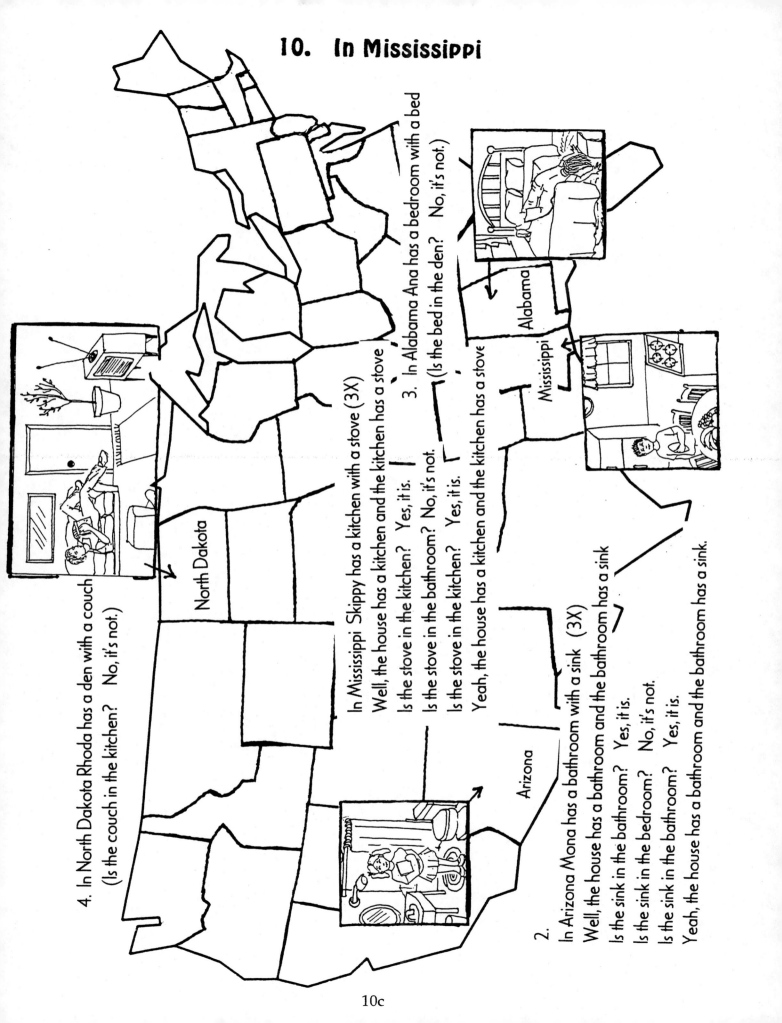

In Mississippi Skippy has a kitchen with a stove (3X)
Well, the house has a kitchen and the kitchen has a stove
Is the stove in the kitchen? Yes, it is.
Is the stove in the bathroom? No, it's not.
Is the stove in the kitchen? Yes, it is.
Yeah, the house has a kitchen and the kitchen has a stove

3. In Alabama Ana has a bedroom with a bed
(Is the bed in the den? No, it's not.)

4. In North Dakota Rhoda has a den with a couch No, it's not.
(Is the couch in the kitchen?

2.
In Arizona Mona has a bathroom with a sink (3X)
Well, the house has a bathroom and the bathroom has a sink
Is the sink in the bathroom? Yes, it is.
Is the sink in the bedroom? No, it's not.
Is the sink in the bathroom? Yes, it is.
Yeah, the house has a bathroom and the bathroom has a sink.

10c

10. In Mississippi

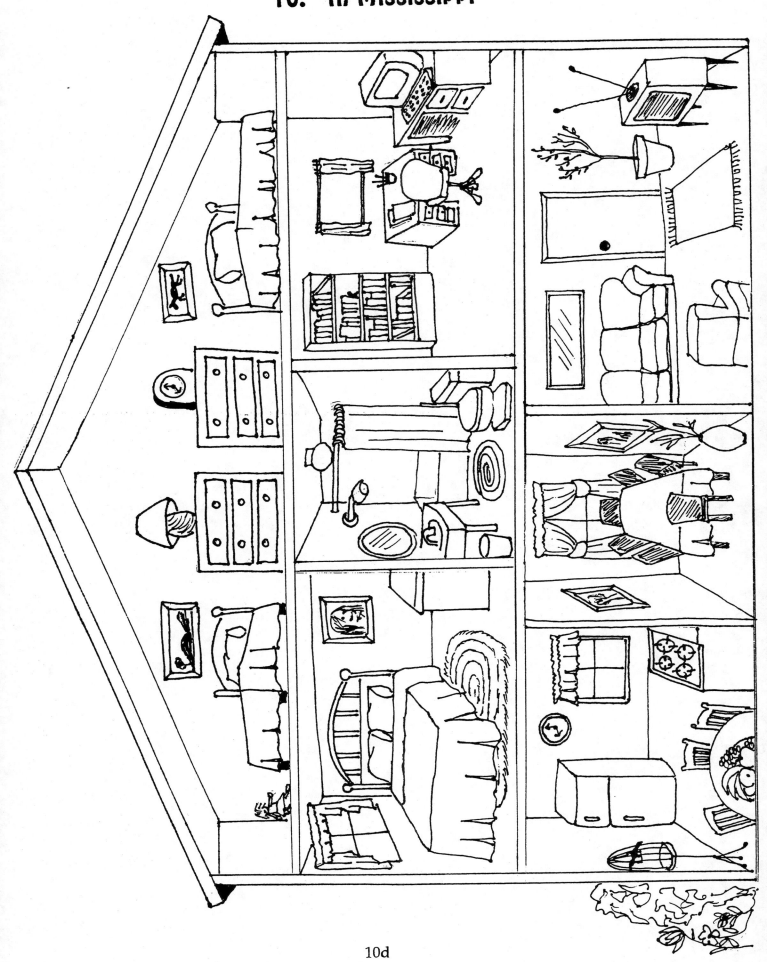

10d

10. In Mississippi

10e

11. Tick Tock

Words and music by Patti Lozano

What's going on? Tell me the time.
Talk about your day and make it rhyme
Talk about the hours and minutes, it's fine
What's going on? Tell me the time.

It's 7:30. I'm getting out of bed
I pull my pajama top over my head.
It's 7:30. I'm getting out of bed,
Hear the tick tock tick tock tick tock tick
It's the music the clock makes all day long

2. It's 10:15, I'm writing on the board
   Language arts is not too hard...

3. It's 3:00, I walk home after school,
   I ride the bus when it's raining, that's the rule...

4. It's 6:45, it's time to eat our food,
   Mom ordered pizza, so she's in a good mood...

5. It's 9:00, I'm getting into bed
   I pull my pajama top over my head...

11a

11. Tick Tock
Teaching Suggestions

Language Objectives:
- ☺ Telling time *(on the hour, half hour and quarter hour)*
- ☺ Talking about a daily routine

Extension Games or Activities:

A. Page 11D is a flashcard page of clocks set at different times and daily activities. The following are several of many ways to use this page.

    1) Make it a worksheet. Students write the correct times below the clocks; then they write correct activities below the illustrations *(i.e. "I am or he/she is playing baseball")*.

    2) Play "Charades Competition." Show a transparency of page 11D and have two colors of translucent sticker dots on hand. (These are available at any office supply store.) Divide students into two teams. The game begins when a student from either team stands at the front of the room and acts out both a time and an activity from the page. The first team to call out the correct time and activity, *(i.e. "It's 10:15. I'm writing on the board")* gets a translucent sticker in their team's color on the corresponding time and activity on the transparency. The team with the most sticker dots on the transparency wins.

    3) Have students cut out the pictures and spread the set in front of them. As they listen to the recording, the hold up the cards that depict the lyrics.

B. As students listen to the recording of the song, have them act out the actions described. They may also be "human clocks," bending one arm at the elbow to be the hour hand.

Modify the Song:

A. Ask students to produce a schedule of a typical day of activities. Try to put it into rhyme to create new verses.

B. Create different verses for students' special days, such as birthdays, Valentine's Day, Field Day, and so on.

11b

11. Tick Tock

What's going on? Tell me the time.
Talk about your day and make it rhyme
Talk about the hours and minutes, it's fine
What's going on? Tell me the time.

It's 7:30. I'm getting out of bed
I pull my pajama top over my head.
It's 7:30. I'm getting out of bed,
Hear the tick tock tick tock tick tock tick
It's the music the clock makes all day long

2. It's 10:15, I'm writing on the board
Language arts is not too hard
It's 10:15, I'm writing on the board
Hear the tick tock tick tock tick tock tick
It's the music the clock makes all day long

3. It's 3:00, I walk home after school,
I ride the bus when it's raining, that's the rule
It's 3:00, I walk home after school,
Hear the tick tock tick tock tick tock tick
It's the music the clock makes all day long

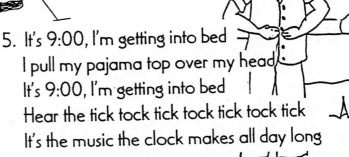

4. It's 6:45, it's time to eat our food,
Mom ordered pizza, so she's in a good mood
It's 6:45, it's time to eat our food,
Hear the tick tock tick tock tick tock tick
It's the music the clock makes all day long

5. It's 9:00, I'm getting into bed
I pull my pajama top over my head
It's 9:00, I'm getting into bed
Hear the tick tock tick tock tick tock tick
It's the music the clock makes all day long

11. Tick Tock

11d

12. Orange Juice

Words and music by Patti Lozano

I don't like to drink sodas, I don't like to drink milk shakes,
And I don't like to drink iced tea or lemonade
I don't like to drink coffee, I don't like to drink water,
I don't like to drink soup hot or cold

Refrain: But I like orange juice for breakfast, orange juice for lunch again,
 Orange juice for dinner with my family
 Orange juice for snacktime, orange juice for bedtime too,
 Orange juice at any time both night and day

I don't like to eat hot dogs, I don't like to eat french fries
And I don't like to eat pizza or hamburgers,
I don't like to eat chicken, I don't like to eat tacos
And I don't like to eat sandwiches at all

12. Orange Juice
Teaching Suggestions

Language Objectives:
- ☺ Popular drinks and foods: *sodas, milk shakes, ice tea, lemonade, coffee, water, soup, orange juice, hot dogs, french fries, pizza, hamburgers, chicken, tacos, sandwiches*
- ☺ Structures: *"I like_____." "I don't like_____."*

Extension Games or Activities:

A. Play "The Telephone." Make a class set of page 12E, if possible printed on different colors of index stock. On the back of each phone write the phone number the child will call. On the front of the phone, write the student's <u>fictional</u> phone number.
IMPORTANT! Every number on the back must correspond with one on the front of another telephone!
Set two chairs back to back in the front of the room. Call the number on the back of your phone. The lucky student who has this phone number comes up to sit in the other chair. Initiate a conversation dealing with foods, drinks and what is liked and not liked.
Teacher: *Ring! Ring! Ring! Ring!*
Student: *Hello?*
Teacher: *Hi, this is Mrs. Parker. Is this Sharon?*
Sharon; *Yes, it is.*
Teacher: *Sharon, I was wondering, do you like hot dogs?*
Student: *No, I don't like hot dogs, but I like hamburgers.*
When they conclude the conversation, the student calls the number on the back of her telephone and the game continues.

Modify the Song:

A. Play with rhyming and extend vocabulary by creating Muddled Lyrics. Alter at least one word in each line of the song so that it becomes ridiculous. Sing it in this manner.
Example: "I don't like to drink sodas, I don't like to drink milk snakes,
And I don't like to drink rice tree or lemonade..."
B. Present a "Dramatic Recitation." Assign each student one phrase of the song and have them illustrate that drink or food item or use the cards on page 12D. They line up in the order of the lyrics and one by one recite their phrase and show their picture.
Example: Student A: I don't like to drink sodas (shows a drawing of a coke)
Student B: I don't like to drink milk shakes....

12b

12. Orange Juice

I don't like to drink sodas, I don't like to drink milk shakes,
And I don't like to drink ice tea or lemonade,
I don't like to drink coffee, I don't like to drink water,
I don't like to drink soup hot or cold

But I like orange juice for breakfast,   Orange juice for lunch again,
Orange juice for dinner with my family
Orange juice for snack time, orange juice for bedtime too,
Orange juice at any time both night and day

I don't like to eat hot dogs, I don't like to eat french fries
And I don't like to eat pizza or hamburgers,
I don't like to eat chicken, I don't like to eat tacos
And I don't like to eat sandwiches at all

But I like orange juice for breakfast,   Orange juice for lunch again,
Orange juice for dinner with my family
Orange juice for snack time, orange juice for bedtime too,
Orange juice at any time both night and day

12. Orange Juice

12. Orange Juice

12e

13. Two Lazy Elephants

Words and music by Patti Lozano

Two lazy elephants were lying in the jungle,
Hiding from the sunlight on a hot summer day
And the larger of the two asked his friend with a sigh,
"What do you want to do?
Where do you want to go?
How do you want to spend the day?"

And he answered:
I want to watch a television show,
I don't want to stay in the jungle anymore
I want to watch a television show
In the village, Come on, let's go!

2. I want to listen to the radio
3. I want to try a new computer game
4. I want to play with puzzles and toys

13a

13. Two Lazy Elephants
Teaching Suggestions

Language Objectives:

- ☺ Leisure time activities: *watch a television show, listen to the radio, try a computer game, play with puzzles and* toys
- ☺ Structures: "I want to _____." "I don't want to _____."
- ☺ Question words and sentences: *"What do you want to do? "Where do you want to go?* " *"How do you want to spend the day?"*

Extension Games or Activities:

A. Play "The Telephone:" Review the instructions and telephone template from pages 12B and 12E. Your conversations this time should revolve around fun and not-so-fun activities. You may want to add *"When...?"* questions to review telling time.

B. Find out from students what their favorite activities are and list them on the board. Make a graph to measure the popularity of the activities. Do the same thing with least favorite activities.

C. Use the vocabulary cards on page 13D to play a variety of activities.
   1) Play "What's Missing?" Make a transparency of the page and give students a few minutes to look closely at the illustrations. Then tell them to close their eyes. Cover one picture with a small square of paper, then allow students to open their eyes and look again. Ask, *"What's missing?"* The student that names the missing picture correctly gets to take the teacher's place and the game continues.
   2) Make a copy of page 13D for each student. Students mill around the class with the sheet and a pencil. They must try to find someone who likes each activity. Find out when and where they do the activity and take notes next to that picture. Share the findings with the class.

Modify the Song:

A. This song makes a cute puppet show with commercially made or paper bag elephants, a jungle backdrop and little cardboard props.
B. Add verses to sing about different animals that don't want to stay in the jungle and what they want to do instead.

13. Two Lazy Elephants

Two lazy elephants were lying in the jungle,
Hiding from the sunlight on a hot summer day
And the larger of the two asked his friend with a sigh,
"What do you want to do?
Where do you want to go?
How do you want to spend the day?"

1. And he answered:
I want to watch a television show,
I don't want to stay in the jungle anymore
I want to watch a television show
In the village, Come on, let's go!

2. "I want to listen to the radio...

3. "I want to try a new computer game...

4. "I want to play with puzzles and toys ...

13. Two Lazy Elephants

13d

14. Oh Irene, Don't Be Mean, Tell Me Please

Words and music by Patti Lozano

Dear Irene, don't be mean, tell me please
Will you go with me tonight to see a movie?
And then after we'll go eat some barbeque and french fries
Dear Irene, don't be mean, tell me please

Oh..... my dearest friend, Bartholomew,
I'd really like to go, but I'm not able to
Please go wash your face and then
You may come and invite me again

2. Please go comb your hair and then
3. Please go brush your teeth and then
4. Please go change your socks and then

14. Dear Irene, Don't Be Mean, Tell Me Please
Teaching Suggestions

Language Objectives:
- ☺ Personal hygiene: *wash your face, comb your hair, brush your teeth, change your socks*
- ☺ Command verb forms

Extension Games or Activities:

A. Use the game board on page 14D to play "Tell Me Quickly!" Distribute a game board to half of the students in the room. The other students only have pencils.

   The students with game boards walk among the students seated with pencils, point to an illustration and identify the command. When the game board student identifies it correctly, the seated student initials that particular picture with a pencil. The game board player may only approach each pencil student one time. The first game board student to have a vertical, horizontal or diagonal row of initials wins. Play again so pencil students have game boards and vice versa.

B. Discuss the plot of this song and the drastic personal hygiene implications. Brainstorm other areas that poor Bartholomew might need to work on before Irene will be seen with him. Place students into small groups to write short plays following this story line. Give each group time to present their play.

Modify the Song:

A. Chant the song instead of singing it and have pairs of students act out the roles of Bartholomew and Irene.

B. This song is a "partner song!" This means both melodies (Bartholomew's and Irene's) may be sung together to create an intricate harmony. Let all boys sing Bartholomew's part while the girls sing Irene's part. (They must know the song very well to do this.)

C. Sing the song cumulatively. With each verse, Irene tacks on an additional thing Bartholomew must do before she will go out with him. (Needless to say, this activity does not work with the cassette.) Have the students pantomime the hygienic actions as they sing about them.

14. Oh Irene, Don't Be Mean, Tell Me Please

Dear Irene, don't be mean, tell me please
Will you go with me tonight to see a movie?
And then after we'll go eat some barbeque
   and french fries
Dear Irene, don't be mean, tell me please

Oh.... my dearest friend, Bartholomew,
I'd really like to go, but I'm not able to
Please go wash your face and then
You may come and invite me again

2. Please go comb your hair and then...

3. Please go brush your teeth and then...

4. Please go change your socks and then...

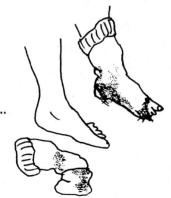

14. Oh Irene, Don't Be Mean, Tell Me Please

Game Board Commands

Wash your face.
Comb your hair.
Brush your teeth.
Change your shoes.
Iron your shirt.

Sit down in the chair.
Listen to the music.
Sing a song.
Take the flower.
Eat the apple.
Close the door.

Draw a triangle.
Write your name.
Count the candies.
Touch the table.
Put on the hat.

15. I Want to See the World in a Fine Purple Car

Words and music by Patti Lozano

I want to see the world in a fine purple car
To travel 'round the country in a fine purple car
I know that I'm too little now, but someday when I'm bigger
I want to see the world in a fine purple car

I don't care if it's shiny, I don't care if it's rusty,
I don't care if it's old or if it's sparkling new
I don't care if it's fast or if it's very slow
But I don't want red or yellow or blue
Only a purple car will do

2. Bus
3. Plane
4. Train

15. I Want to See the World in a Fine Purple Car
Teaching Suggestions

Language Objectives:
- ☺ Transportation: *car, bus, plane, train*
- ☺ Adjectives: *fine, purple, shiny, rusty, old, sparkling, new, fast, slow, red, yellow, blue*

Extension Games or Activities:

A. Use the transportation flash cards on page 15D to play a variety of games:
1. Play "Team Charades:" Divide the class into two teams and choose a leader for each team. Give each leader one set of transportation cards, shuffled so that each deck is in a different order. The leader pantomimes each mode of transportation. See which team can correctly identify all the cards first.
2. Use a large map of the world to plan a hypothetical trip across the continents. Use dot stickers to label each destination. Use peel-off correction tape to mark the route taken. Place transpiration flash cards to mark each chosen method of travel. Give all students turns to plan one destination and mode of travel.
3. Play "Bubbles:" Blow a wand of bubbles and see how many methods of transportation volunteers can name from page 15D before the last bubble pops!

Modify the Song:

A. Chant the lyrics with different emotions, such as angry, frightened, spoiled, sad. As always when chanting, keep a steady beat with two fingers.

B. Chant the song in a two-part round. Group 2 should begin four beats after group 1.

C. Advanced activity: Isolate parts of speech, one at a time. (This is tricky at first, but it's lots of fun — and it reinforces parts of speech at the same time!
1. Chant the words but clap the adjectives.
2. Chant the words but stomp the nouns.
3. Chant the words but snap the verbs.
4. Do all of the above together!

15. I Want to See the World in a Fine Purple Car

I want to see the world in a fine purple car
To travel 'round the country in a fine purple car
I know that I'm too little now, but someday when I'm bigger
I want to see the world in a fine purple car

I don't care if it's shiny, I don't care if it's rusty,

I don't care if it's old or if it's sparkling new

I don't care if it's fast or if it's very slow

But I don't want red or yellow or blue
Only a purple car will do

2. I want to see the world in a fine purple bus
   To travel 'round the country in a fine purple bus
   I know that I'm too little now, but someday when I'm bigger
   I want to see the world in a fine purple bus

3. I want to see the world in a fine purple plane
   To travel 'round the country in a fine purple plane
   I know that I'm too little now, but someday when I'm bigger
   I want to see the world in a fine purple plane

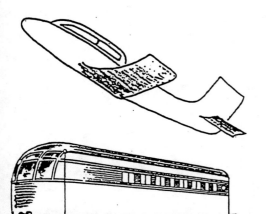

4. I want to see the world in a fine purple train
   To travel 'round the country in a fine purple train
   I know that I'm too little now, but someday when I'm bigger
   I want to see the world in a fine purple train

15. I Want to See the World in a Fine Purple Car

15d

Teacher Guide to Page "d" and "e"
Activity Templates and Flashcards

1d. Two-dimensional "radio" to play "The Radio Game"
   One radio must be colored and assembled according to instructions on page 1d

2d. Name card
   Prepare a class set according to instructions on page 2b

3d and 3e. The letters of the alphabet
   Contains all twentysix letters plus extra letters: a, e, o, l, n, p, r, s, t
   Also contains one blank flashcard, a "magic letter," which can stand in for any letter

4d. Classroom flashcards
   pencil, chalkboard, teacher, table, students, paper, scissors, ruler, calendar, crayon, book, trashcan and trash

5d. Classroom activities or classroom TPR commands
   draw a square, color (or draw) a picture, write your name
   clap your hands, read a book, do a math problem (or write on the board)
   do a science experiment (or study science), talk with your friend, sing a song
   cut with scissors, play a game, answer a question (or raise your hand)

6d. Body part flashcards
   face, head, eyes
   nose, mouth (also teeth and lips), ear
   hair, neck (also chin), shoulder (also chest)
   arm (also elbow), fingers (also hand), back (also waist)
   legs, knee, foot (also toes)

7d. Clothing flashcards
   shirt (also T-shirt), pants, socks
   shoes, jacket, dress
   skirt, blouse, sweater
   shorts, hat, underwear

Teacher Guide to Page "d" and "e"
Activity Templates and Flashcards *(continued)*

8d. Bird template

Prepare according to instructions on page 8b

9d. Family flashcards

mother, father, sister (and daughter), brother (and son)
grandmother (or grandma), grandfather (or grandpa), pet dog, pet cat

10d. House poster

Living room contains: television, rug, arm chair, couch (or sofa), door, mirror, plant
Dining room contains: table, chairs, curtains, window
Kitchen contains: refrigerator, birdcage, table, chairs, window, stove, clock
Home office contains: desk, computer, bookshelf
Bathroom contains: toilet, sink, mirror, shower (and bathtub), light, rug, trashcan
Bedrooms contain: beds, rug, dresser, lamp, clock, paintings

10e. Contains reduced family members to place in house poster for various games and activities

11d. Clocks show times highlighted in song: 7:30, 10:15, 3:00, 6:45, 9:00
Extra clocks: 1:25, 8:50, 4:10
Activities (highlighted in song): I'm getting out of bed.   (He's getting out of bed.)
I'm writing on the board. (He's writing on the board.)
I'm walking home after school. (He's walking home...)
I'm eating pizza for dinner.   (He's eating pizza...)
I'm getting into bed.   (He's getting into bed.)
Extra daily activities: I'm reading a book.   I'm playing the guitar. I'm playing basketball.

12d. Food flashcards

orange juice (and oranges), sodas (bottles and cans), milk shake (with a straw)
coffee, soup (and crackers), hot dog
french fries (also salt and pepper), pizza, hamburger
chicken, taco, sandwich
grapes, ice cream (ice cream cone), apple

12e. Telephone template

Prepare according to instructions on page 12b

Teacher Guide to Page "d" and "e"
Activity Templates and Flashcards *(continued)*

13d. Leisure activity flashcards
  I want to... watch a television show   listen to the radio
    work on the computer (or play a computer game) play with puzzles and toys
    bake cookies   play the guitar
    play soccer   play a video game

14d. Game Board for personal hygiene and other activities and commands
  All commands are identified on the bottom of page 14d
  Directions to play the game, "Tell Me Quickly!" are on page 14b.

15d. Transportation flash cards
  car, bus, plane (or airplane or jet)
  boat (or sailboat), bicycle, elephant
  horse, balloon (or hot air balloon), truck
  motorcycle, train, "on foot"

Notes